"I have seen hundreds of silhouettes.
I have had my profile cut numerous times.
But now, for the first time, I feel that I know how
to get started learning to cut profiles freehand.
Kathryn Flocken's new book, Silhouettes: Rediscovering
the Lost Art, is a welcome addition to the very limited
literature on silhouette cutting."

Steven Woodbury,
Book Review Editor, First Cut
(magazine of the Guild of American Paper Cutters)

"This book is the most detailed and accurate instruction
on the art of cutting silhouettes that I have ever seen in
print. I wish I had it when I first started learning! This
book is like looking over the shoulder of an experienced
silhouette artist."

Alexandria Skordas,
Practicing the art of silhouettes for over 25 years… and counting!

"Kathryn's book is the ultimate 'how-to' on silhouettes
ever published. A definite professional guide."

Vincent Totera,
Professional Silhouette Artist

SILHOUETTES:
Rediscovering the Lost Art

SILHOUETTES:
Rediscovering the Lost Art

A Step-By-Step Guide
to the Art of Silhouette Portraiture

Kathryn K. Flocken

First Edition

Published by PaperPortraits.com Press
Edited by Deborah B. Adams

Manufactured in the United States of America.
Library of Congress Card Number: 00-104261
ISBN: 0-9701151-0-5
Illustrations: Kathryn K. Flocken
Design/Production: Berto Henríquez
Photography: Jenn McIntyre
Cover design: Kathryn K. Flocken

Send all inquiries to:
PaperPortraits.com
c/o Kathryn K. Flocken
P.O. Box 547812
Orlando, FL 32854-7812
email: kathyart@earthlink.net
website: www.paperportraits.com

*This book is dedicated
to my husband, Berto*

CONTENTS

PREFACE

In this modern age of photography, film and digital art, silhouette portraiture and design is fast becoming a lost art. The purpose of this book is to share the professional methods and techniques of this original artistry with the hope that it will live on as a classic art form for generations to come.

ACKNOWLEDGMENTS

Special thanks to all who posed for portraits and agreed to have their image or their child's image shown in my book. Thanks to Vincent Totera, Alexandria Skordas, Irina Zakharova, Ed Sanderson, Dean Montalbano, Dessy Henriquez, and the late Rico Prosperoso for your artistic contributions. Thank you Jenn McIntyre for your friendship and photography skills. The Queen of Commas would like to thank Deborah B. Adams, for, your, editing, skills. Thanks Mom and Dad for the tremendous gift of higher education and believing I'd make something of my life with or without it. Thanks Mom, for not minding (even though the teacher did) that I drew waterfalls on my math papers as a kid. Thank you to my cousin, author James A. Michener for the inspiration to strive for greatness and to leave my mark on the world. Thank you Berto for your love, kindness, support, and artistic talents lent to the making of this book. I couldn't have done it without you. I love you.

INTRODUCTION

The art of silhouette portraiture is an unforgiving one and can be very challenging at first. Just like any form of artwork, it takes practice, perseverance, and patience -- lots and lots of patience. Everyone is different and has their own learning curve. How fast you master the art of silhouette depends largely on your artistic skill level and the amount of practice you're willing to put into it. Eventually, given time and experience, you will perfect your craft.

Silhouette cutting is a form of drawing. Instead of using a pen or pencil as your drawing tools, however, you are using scissors. If you can draw what you see using a pencil, you should be able to cut silhouettes once you learn the basic techniques laid out in this book. The secret is in learning to control and manipulate your scissors. Best of all, there are two saving graces to silhouette portraiture. If you cut a feature too large, you can simply trim it down. Or, if the silhouette is completely beyond repair, you can simply start over. After all, it only takes minutes to achieve a portrait and pennies worth of paper. In the end, you will have created a beautiful, personalized keepsake for your subject. What better gift to give or receive!

Just remember, practice does make perfect. No matter what your silhouettes look like at first, whether they are for sale or just for fun, keep practicing and don't get discouraged. Your first tries are apt to be crude -- possibly not even human looking. My first silhouettes resembled the statues on Easter Island! But, in less than three months, I was cutting silhouettes and getting paid to do it! If you keep at it, you, too, will eventually achieve the results you want. I did, and so can you!

As an added bonus, you will find helpful hints noted with this scissor icon ✄ sprinkled throughout the entire book. Happy cutting!

Kathryn Flocken

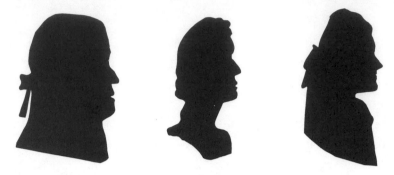

These are some first-time silhouettes done by 12-year-old Dessy Henriquez.

Left: One of my own early efforts with a few weeks practice. Center: Silhouette by Dean Montalbano. Right: Silhouette by Ed Sanderson.

First-time silhouette by Melanie, from Austria.

✂ As Unique as Fingerprints. Just as everyone's fingerprints, handwriting and drawing styles are different, each artist's silhouettes will look different, too. Note the individual styles of the various artist's work included within this book, and realize that your silhouettes will have a unique look of their own as well. Your style will constantly develop, change and improve within the first year of doing silhouette portraits. Keep some of your earliest attempts at the art form to measure your improvement.

Clarissa draws her scissors from the case,
To draw the lines of poor Dan Jackson's face.
One sloping line cut forehead, nose and chin,
A nick produced a mouth and made him grin.
-Jonathan Swift

CHAPTER ONE
SILHOUETTES: A BRIEF HISTORY

There are two types of silhouettes, both cut with scissors from black paper. The first type is called "scherenschnitte" which is a German word meaning "scissor cut." These highly detailed, lace-like paper designs began as a traditional craft in 19th century Europe in Germany, Austria, and Switzerland and quickly became a popular art form. Some scherenschnitte paper designs are cut strictly from the imagination of the artist directly onto the paper without the aid of pen or ink. Others are created from original drawings or pre-made patterns. Regardless how the scherenschnitte is achieved, it demands high levels of both patience and skill to create. Limited only by his or her imagination, the professional scherenschnitte artist can capture a myriad of beautiful and unique silhouette shapes, scenes, and intricate patterns of design.

The second type of silhouette is the silhouette portrait. This form of portraiture became popular in the mid-1700s in France through the artistic talents of its namesake, French bureaucrat Etienne de Silhouette.

A precursor to the modern-day photograph, the silhouette was a favorite way for all classes of society, from royalty to common folk, to capture the likeness of family members and loved ones for posterity. Silhouette portraits were also an inexpensive alternative to the more extravagant commissioned oil portraits. To this day, silhouette portraits are still referred to as the "poor man's portrait."

Most professional silhouette artists create their portraits the authentic way by using scissors and black paper. The subject sits and poses for a matter of minutes while the artist cuts out the subject's profile freehand with a pair of scissors. But, silhouette portraiture isn't just for the professionals. Amateur silhouette artists of the past would trace their subject's image with a machine called the *camera obscura*. Today amateurs can easily make excellent life-size silhouette profiles with the method school teachers use. With this method you simply use a projector and a darkened room to cast the subject's shadow on the wall and then trace it and cut it out. For an even simpler approach, the same effect can be achieved by using a flashlight.

Above are are two fine examples of silhouette portraits. They are Martha and George Washington. Below and at right, two examples of scheren-schnitte, most likely done from a drawing first, then later cut out.

CHAPTER TWO
MATERIALS NEEDED

You may or may not need all of the items listed below depending upon whether you choose to cut silhouette portraits as a hobby or for a profession.

BASIC ESSENTIALS

Scissors: You will need a pair of surgical scissors with a short blade and long handle. At first you can practice with an inexpensive pair of cuticle scissors or a pair of scherenschnitte scissors. If you treat your scissors well, they will rarely need sharpening. Your silhouette scissors can be sent back to the surgical supply company to be sharpened, or just take them to a knife shop to be sharpened. Scissors and paper supplies are offered on page 164.

Silhouette Paper: Black French silhouette paper cut to 5"x8." To order in quantity see the supplies list on page 164. This paper is not easy to find and usually must be ordered in bulk quantity if you go directly through a paper supplier.

White Paper: You can purchase plain white 4-ply paper at either a local art supply store or in bulk at a local paper supplier. Cut the paper into 5"x7" sheets or tell the paper supplier cut it when placing your order.

Newsprint: You need plain newsprint cut into 5"x7" sheets. If you don't want to cut your own, you can find it at art supply stores or through paper suppliers. This paper is used up to blot up excess glue in the paste-up process.

Tape: You need clear or masking tape to make your own burnishing tool. Refer to the Paste-Up section on page 113 to learn how to make this simple blotting tool.

Glue: A cellulose based dry powder wallpaper paste is best to use. Wall paper paste is convenient because it can be mixed and stored in small quantities. Rubber cement may also be used, but be aware that it hardens quickly if the jar is left open for long periods of time. Another problem is that rubber cement will yellow the paper over a period of time.

Water: To mix with glue.

UTENSILS

Attractive Container for Paste: For the best presentation, purchase a small brass pot or a barber's shaving cream mug to mix and store glue.

Brush: Use a 1 1/2" paintbrush from the hardware store or a barber's shaving cream brush. Paint brushes made with animal hair work better than plastic bristled paint brushes.

Spoon: To measure paste and stir glue.

Pen: Choose a black ink pen or calligraphy pen for personalizing and signing the portraits.

BOOTH SETUP

Chairs: You will need two chairs of the same height -- one for you and one for your subject. You may even want to purchase a booster chair for small children to help raise them up closer to your eye level.

Table: You will need a table that is large enough to hold supplies and do paste-up.

Lights: Be kind to your eyesight. Good lighting is a must, whether it is indoor lighting, sunshine, or portable lights that clamp onto your table. Be sure to carry lots of extension cords.

Children's Book: This is your "secret weapon" to settle down an active child. Be sure it's a sturdy, hard-bound book with lots of bright colorful pictures to hold the child's attention.

SALES PRODUCTS

Frames: These are optional, but a real sales booster. You can purchase inexpensive, but attractive 5"x7" square or oval frames from any craft store or wholesale dealer. Black or brass looks best with silhouettes.

Mats: These are optional, but make a nice border to complement, as well as protect, the silhouette.

Courtesy Bags: These bags are to hold your customer's sales items.

CHAPTER THREE
GETTING STARTED

Before you begin cutting silhouette portraits, there are some basic exercises to practice in order to learn how to manipulate the scissors. This chapter will also show you how to fold the paper, hold the paper, hold the scissors, and have good posture while cutting the portrait.

GETTING USED TO THE SCISSORS

Practice the following exercise to familiarize yourself with the feel of the scissors. Control and confidence will increase the more you practice these basic shapes and cuts.

Hold the scissors with your thumb and middle finger for maximum control when cutting. Slightly slant the blades of the scissors in order to see the shapes you are cutting. Remember to cut on the white side of the paper so you can see what you are doing.

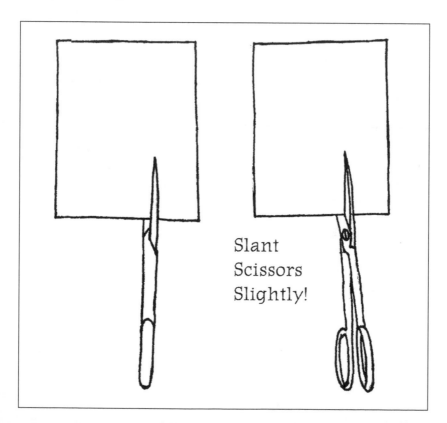

Slant
Scissors
Slightly!

Practice cutting these shapes over and over. Start from the bottom of the paper and work your way to the top -- twisting and turning the paper with your non-dominant hand. Your non-dominant hand works as a guide to turn the paper in the needed directions. It also holds the paper steadily. Start by cutting slowly and be aware of your control. You may want to fold the paper in two to prevent the scissors from sliding and ripping the paper. Practice on typing paper and save your silhouette paper.

Beginners Tip. When you feel comfortable with the scissors, start practicing your portraits on live subjects such as family members and friends. You can also take clear profile photographs from the bust up, and practice cutting those. If cutting from a photograph, prop it up or tape it to the wall.

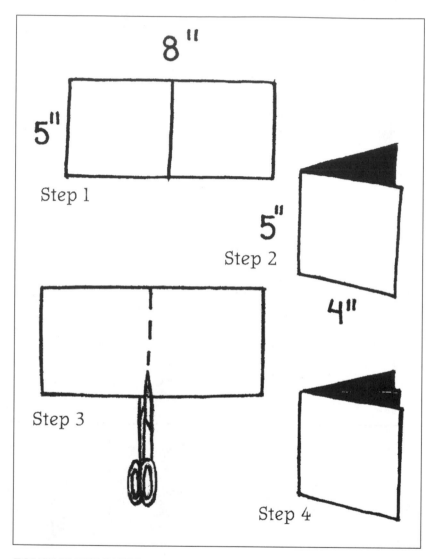

8"

5"

Step 1

5"

Step 2

4"

Step 3

Step 4

FOLDING THE PAPER

Fold the silhouette paper in two, with the black on the inside and white on the outside. Only stack and fold two or three sheets at a time so the edges of the paper meet perfectly. If the edges are left uneven, part of the silhouette could be cut off inadvertently, leaving the subject with a flat nose or head.

Next, fold and cut sheets of silhouette paper in half. Then, insert the half-sheets into the folded pieces. The end result will be the silhouette done in triplicate.

POSTURE AND HOLDING THE PAPER

As a silhouette artist, you will be sitting for long periods of time, so try to maintain the best posture possible. Sit with your back straight and check your posture often throughout your sessions. When cutting a small child's portrait, have the child sit in a booster chair or on the lap of a parent to raise the child up closer to your eye level.

Above: Correct posture and way to hold paper. Bottom: Incorrect posture and way to hold paper.

Next, hold the paper vertically in front of you at about chin or breast level. Keep the paper approximately 12 inches from your face. The subject's head should be at eye level. Your eyes should constantly move back and forth from subject to paper. Resist temptation to hold the paper flat on your lap! The portrait will be distorted if you do so and probably won't look at all like the subject.

HOLDING THE PAPER AND SCISSORS

If you are right-handed, hold the paper in your left hand at the fold. Holding the paper at the fold helps prevent it from falling apart at mid-cut. Have the subject sit in a chair in front of you about one to two feet away. Then, cut the subject's right profile.

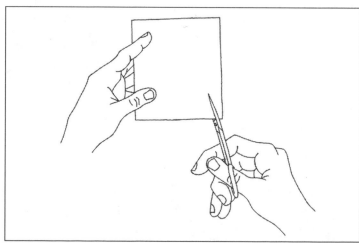

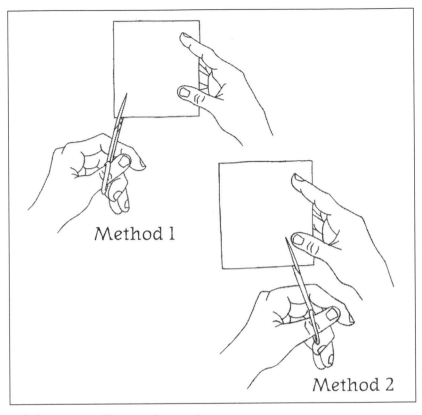

Method 1

Method 2

Lefties can cut silhouettes in one of two ways:

1. Hold the paper in your right hand at the fold. Cut the subject's left profile. Left-handed scissors are required.

2. Hold the paper in your right hand at the loose end of the paper and cut the subject's right profile. You may find the previous method less awkward, but try both ways and see what suits you best. For this method, you may use right-handed scissors.

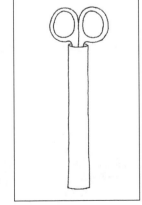

Safety First. Make a protective sheath for your scissors and always keep them out of the reach of children. Use one 5x7 piece of white 4-ply paper and some tape to fashion the sheath.

CHAPTER FOUR
BASIC ANATOMY

When drawing a portrait with pencil, you may begin anywhere -- at the nose, the outline of the face, or an eye. The nice part is that construction lines may be made and mistakes can be erased.

Silhouettes differ from pencil portraits in that you must begin at a certain spot, no construction lines can be made, and there is virtually no erasing of any mistakes whatsoever.

In order for you to minimize your mistakes, you should enter the art form with some amount of drawing ability and a very basic knowledge of anatomy.

Here is a refresher course in anatomy, with Abraham Lincoln and George Washington as models.

The base of the nose is half-way between the eyes and the chin.

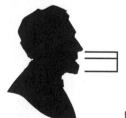

The mouth is 1/3 of the way down from the base of the nose to the chin.

When the head is divided into two equal parts, a line bisects the lower eye lid.

The lower half of the face can again be divided equally, marking the top of the lip.

The length from the top of the head to the chin equals the width from the tip of the nose to the back of the head.

In many faces, a slanted line can be made from the tip of the nose touching the upper lip, lower lip, and chin.

The nape of the neck is directly across from the area between the chin and bottom lip. Measure this area carefully at all times, remembering the thickness of the neck denotes the subject's age and weight.

Special consideration should be taken for the anatomical differences in infants and small children as compared to adults.

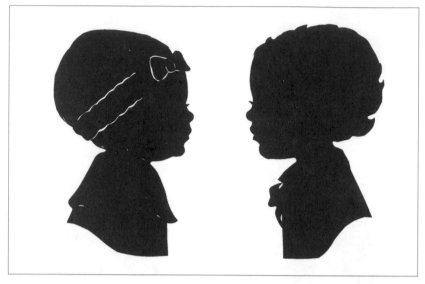

An infant's head is more oval shaped and elongated, with the widest area of the head above the ears. Infants' eyes fall lower on the face, and the forehead is full and protrudes to some degree. The facial bones and jaw bones are small, and the bridge of the nose has not yet developed. The neck is thin and short in comparison with the size of the head.

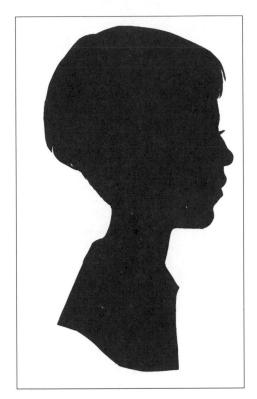

As a child develops, the face lengthens and loses its roundness. The nose becomes more prominent with the development of the bridge bone. Baby teeth and then permanent teeth add width and depth at the lower part of the face. The jaw bone becomes more angular and pointed, and the chin becomes more squared. The neck becomes longer, and the body becomes more proportionate to the size of the head.

Keep Quiet. Try not to speak while cutting a portrait. Talking detracts from your focus. Make sure the subject does not speak, laugh, or smile, as all of these things tend to distort the anatomy of the face, which can make your job all the more difficult.

CHAPTER FIVE
CUTTING THE SILHOUETTE

A silhouette portrait is more or less a series of measured and controlled curves with only a few flat planes. A silhouette artist's job is to take these shapes and curves one by one and create a whole picture from them. In fact, too many straight lines can make for a very stiff looking portrait. The goal of a silhouette artist is to inject muscle, anatomy, personality and life into each portrait.

Cutting silhouettes is a two-step process. First you will focus on a particular feature of the subject's profile -- its individual shape and form -- concentrating your attention on only one feature at a time. Second, you will cut out that feature. For example, look at the chin -- then cut the chin. Look at the lips -- then cut the lips.

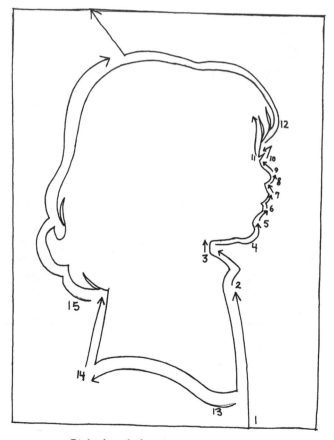

Right-handed artist cutting sequence

Look at the nose -- then cut the nose. Your gaze will constantly go back and forth from subject to paper, subject to paper, until the silhouette is completed. A good silhouette artist can complete a silhouette in about 90 seconds or less.

Here are sample silhouettes with each step of the cutting process in numerical order for both left and right-handed artists. Following this illustration, each step is explained in detail individually.

(NOTE: All steps are explained from the right-handed perspective. Remember Lefties: You should begin from the lower left-hand corner of the paper and work from the subject's left profile).

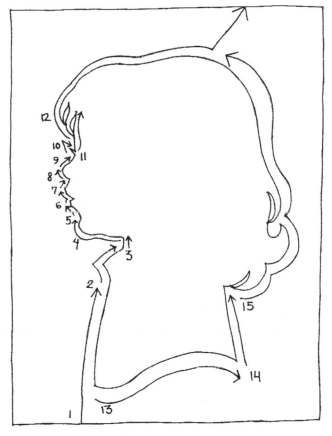

Left-handed artist cutting sequence

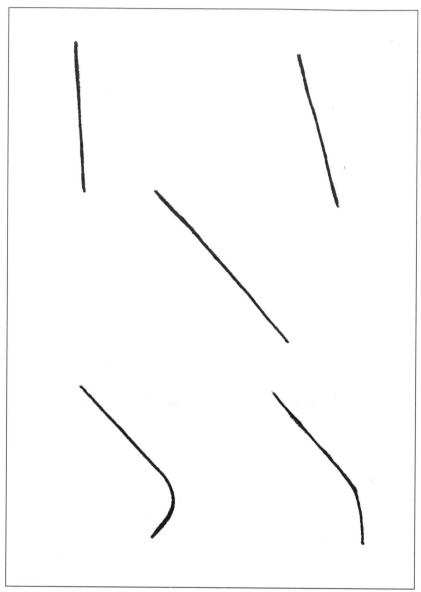

1. The Chest Wall: This shape coincides with the front of the chest, beginning at the bust and moving upwards toward the neck. Start at the lower right-hand corner of the paper. Remember to keep in mind the subject's weight, age, and body shape.

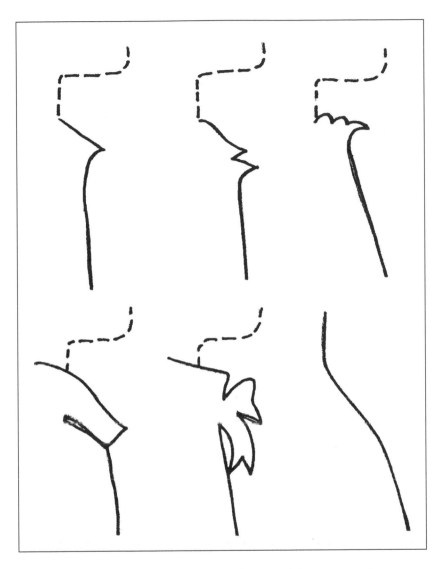

2. The Collar: Make a collar for your subject as elaborate or as plain as you wish. The collar can also be a reflection of the clothing the person is wearing at the moment. The best rule of thumb is to keep it simple and focus on making an accurate portrait. Keep in mind that the main purpose of a silhouette is to capture the subject's personality rather than the clothes or every loose strand of hair. Look ahead at step 13 (the Cameo) for further collar ideas to practice.

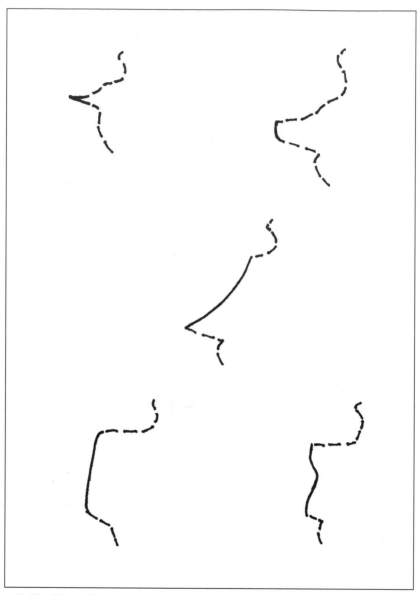

3. The Neck: The neck is a very important indicator of age and weight. Start by focusing on the shape and length of the neck only. Isolate the shape. Then ask yourself the following questions: Is the neck short, medium or long? Is there a slope to it or perhaps an Adam's Apple?

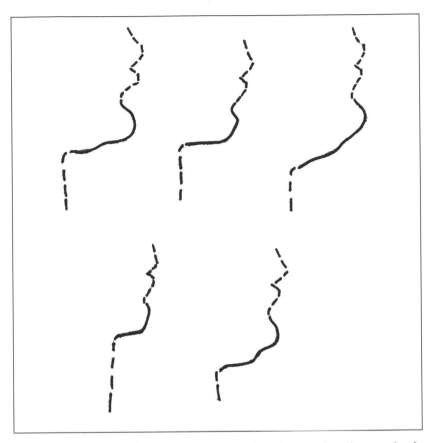

4. The Chin: Isolate this area, focusing on chin shape and attributes only. Is there fatty tissue under the chin? How pronounced is it? Is there a long, sloping neck with nearly no chin at all? Is it squared off or rounded?

"Plastic Surgery." Under the chin is the most requested feature on which to do a little surgery. Trim the least amount of fatty tissue off the portrait as possible. Altering a subject's appearance too much can backfire and ruin your portrait. The subject may protest, "It doesn't even look like me !" And, of course it won't. It is what they wish they looked like!

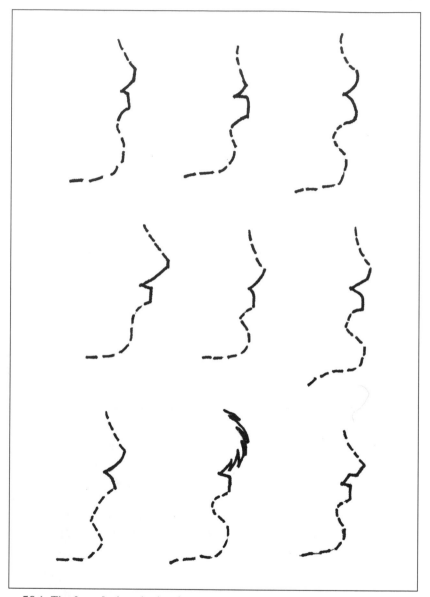

5&6. The Lips: Isolate the lips by cutting one at a time. Step 5 is the lower lip, and step 6 is the upper lip. Look for flat planes on the lips and study their shape and relation closely. Does the upper lip stick out further than the lower one or vice versa? Are the lips full or thin? Is one full while the other is thin?

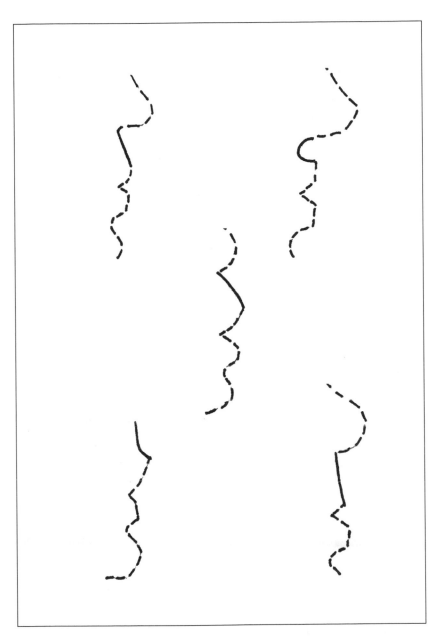

7. The Philtrum: Is the shape between the top of the lip and the nose long or short? Does it curve in or out? Is it straight? Or is it slightly slanted back?

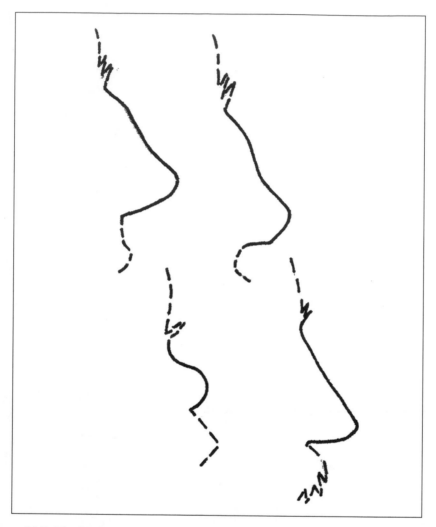

8&9. The Nose: The nose is the most important feature to portray correctly because it defines the personality. Cut the nose slowly and in two steps.

Step 8 is the underside of the nose and sets up the basic shape. Be sure to look at the length and angle in which it slopes. Is it a down-turned nose or does it slope upwards? Is it straight out or perhaps straight out with a slightly upturned tip? Is the area short or long? Are there any flat planes? Is the tip rounded, squared, or pointed?

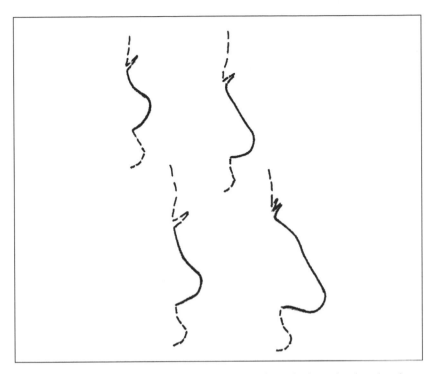

Step 9 is the bridge of the nose. Watch the angle and take it slowly. Are there bumps on the nose, ski slopes, or hooks? How short or long is the nose? Is the bridge of the nose developed yet?

The more distinct the nose, the easier it is to capture in silhouette. Remember, however, to cut this feature very carefully keeping in mind that it is not a cartoon caricature! Even the most subtle cut can change the portrait dramatically. Strive for a realistic portrait without exaggerated features.

If the nose is cut too large, it can be trimmed down carefully within reason. If the nose or any other feature is cut too small, however, or an angle is cut entirely wrong, you must begin again. Do your best work because people notice and comment on the nose more than any other feature in the silhouette.

Be sure to watch proportions and anatomy! If the nose is cut too deep forcing the forehead too far back, the portrait will have a "mutt face" like a dog with a snout.

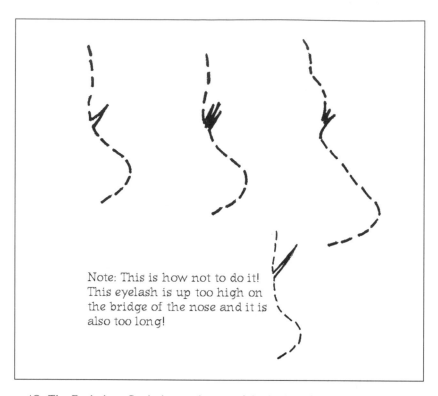

Note: This is how not to do it!
This eyelash is up too high on
the bridge of the nose and it is
also too long!

10. The Eyelashes: Cut lashes at the top of the bridge of the nose, but not too high. Cut a delicate single lash or make a few snips for multiple lashes. Be sure not to make lashes too thick or too long. Put lashes on all subjects, even adult males. You may even want to put eyebrow hairs on some adult males for added detail and masculinity.

Repairing a "Cut-Off" Eyelash. This happens often when first learning to cut silhouettes. Cut an extra long "eyelash" from scrap silhouette paper and glue it partially under the silhouette at the top of the bridge of the nose. Have the pointed tip of the lash showing while the extra length is anchored under the silhouette.

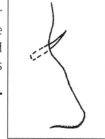

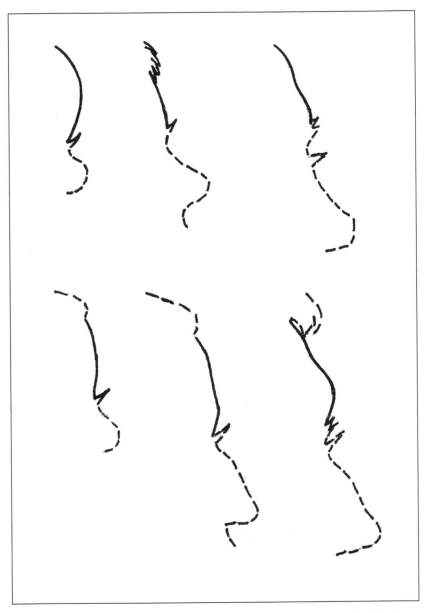

11. The Forehead: Isolate the shape and look at the angle and length of the forehead. Is there a pronounced brow bone? Is it a flat or rounded forehead? Are there ridges?

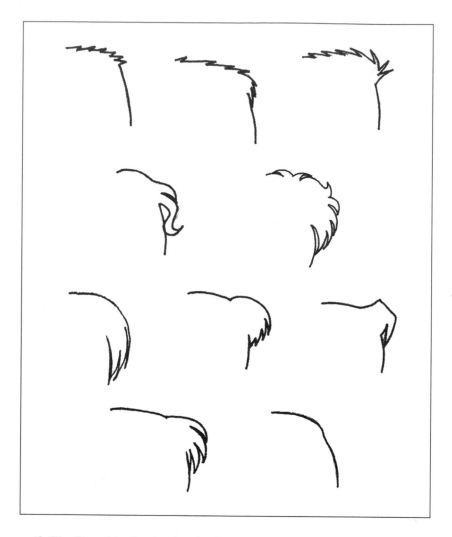

12. The Top of the Forehead to the Crown: Practice different hairstyles and be sure to make the shape of the subject's cranium correct. Watch carefully to see which direction the hair lies on the head. This is especially important for males with buzz cuts. Bald heads must be cut perfectly because there is no hair to hide the shape of the skull.

Once you have completed this step, cut the loose paper out of the way and move on to the cameo as the next step.

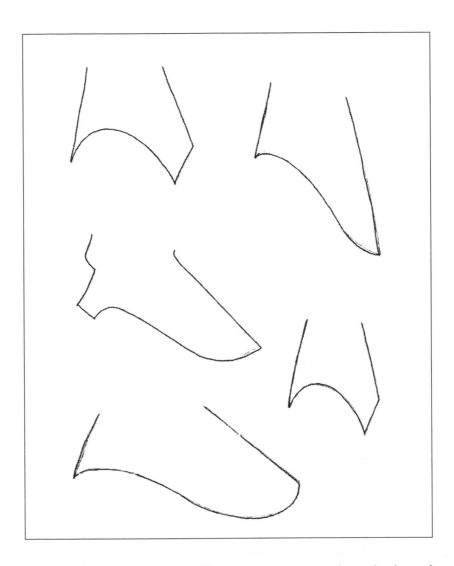

13. The Cameo: Make a simple "S" curve or be creative and vary the shape of the cameo as desired. Before cutting off the cameo completely, look at the length of the subject's hair (look at all subjects for multiples). If a subject has long hair, compensate for hair length by cutting off only half of the cameo, leaving some space on the paper for hair to flow down the back. Also be sure to keep the subject's body shape and weight in mind as you create the width of the cameo. The wider the cameo, the heavier the subject will appear in the final outcome.

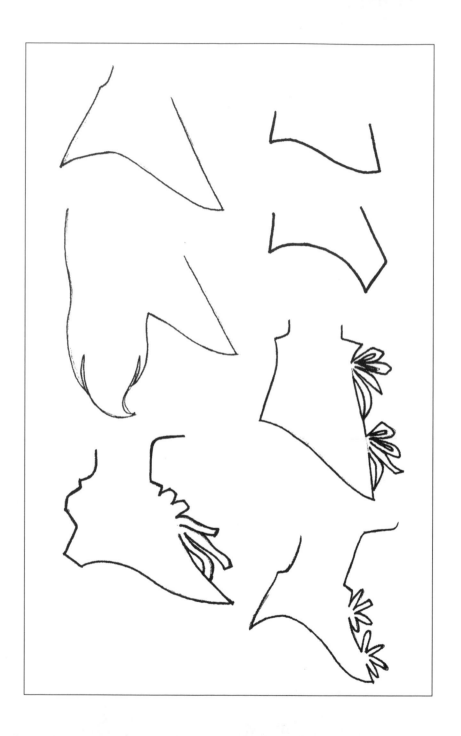

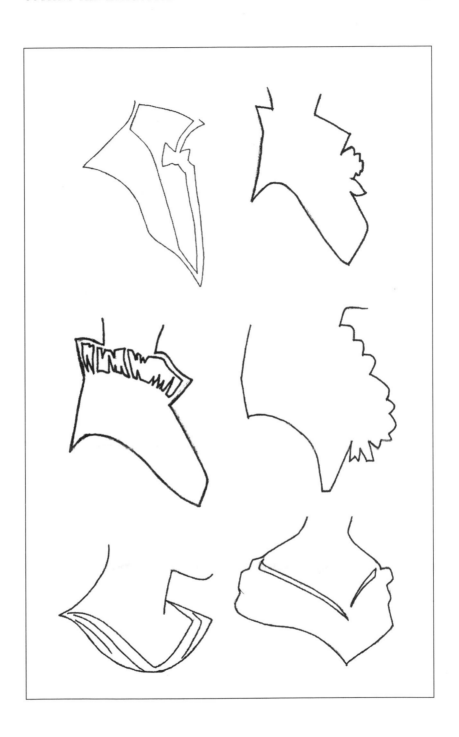

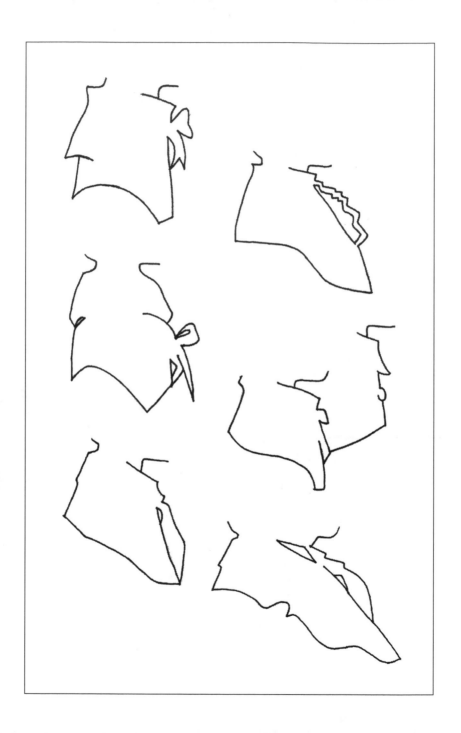

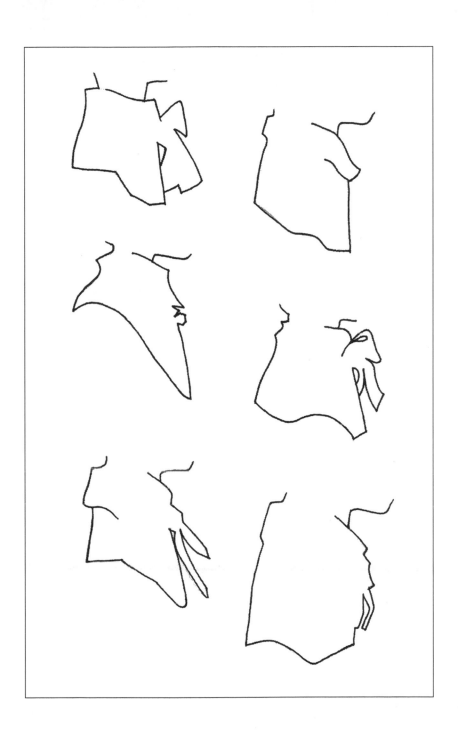

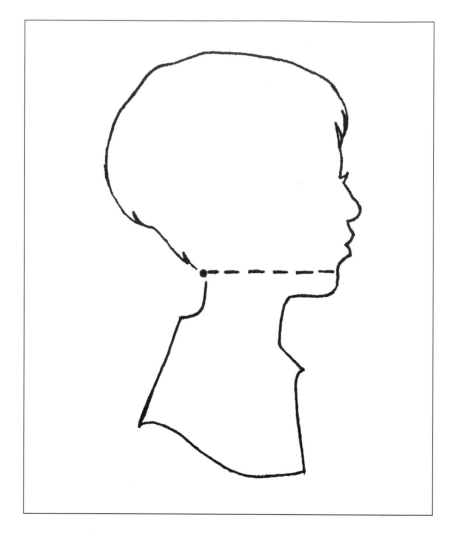

14. The Back to the Nape of the Neck: Keep the subject's body shape, neck width, and hairstyle in mind as you cut up the back to the neck area. Both body width and neck width are important indicators of age and weight.

Measure the width of the neck. The nape of the neck should line up across from the midpoint between the chin and lower lip. For more accuracy, make a tiny indentation in the paper with the scissors at the nape of the neck. Aim for this indentation while cutting up the back. The proportions should be just right.

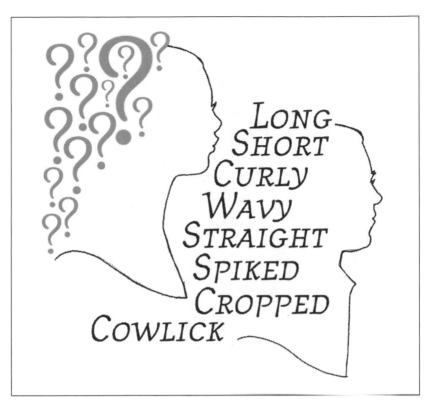

15. The Hair: When making hair, always look to see where it falls on the subject's body. Is the hair to the nape of the neck? Shoulder length? Middle of the back? To the belt? What is the shape, texture, and style of the hair?

Begin by cutting upwards following the shape of the hair until you reach the top of the head. If you measured correctly, the cut will meet perfectly where you left off at step 12. If you make the shape of the head too large or egg-like, just shave some of the excess paper away as needed.

Put in details and "slices of light" as the very last step. Simply make an initial cut, then cut a tiny sliver of paper away to reveal some white-space that will show through once you paste the silhouette down.

Chapter 6 will go into greater detail , showing a myriad of haistyles, hair textures, bows, hats and glasses.

HAIR STYLES, BOWS, HATS AND GLASSES

Straight hair: Make sure you don't cut stiff and static hair. Even straight hair flows. The shape of the hair adds life and movement to the portrait and is all-important in the overall effect of the picture.

Curly hair: Practice cutting plenty of curls and wavy shapes. Echo what type of curls the subject has by making either tight tiny curls, ringlets or thick waves with curly flips at the bottom. Follow the outline of the subject's hair and cut out any distinct shapes that add personality and "soul" to the portrait.

Extra long hair: For girls with extra long hair, cut the hair in a curved shape beneath the cameo. Try to cut the portrait as high up on the paper as possible to maximize the amount of space you have at the bottom for hair.

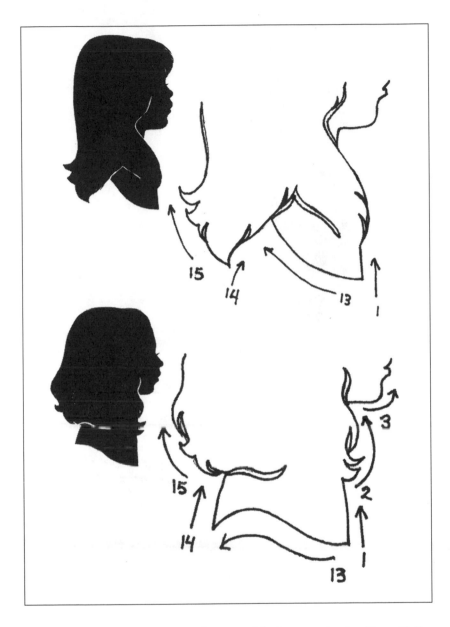

Hair over the shoulder: Show only some of the hair over the shoulder, with the rest left in back. This technique works very nicely in multiple subject silhouettes that feature more than one female in the group.

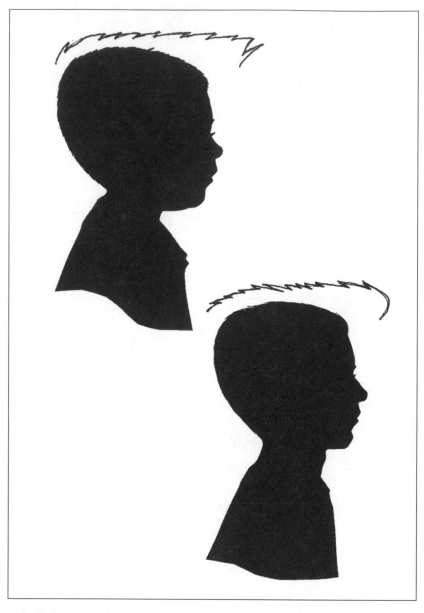

Spiked hair: Cut the spikes in the same direction they fall on the subject's head. Follow the shape of the skull carefully, as buzz-cuts will usually conform tightly to the shape of the cranium.

Bowl-cut: Watch where the bowl-cut begins. Does the bowl-cut start at the bottom of the head like a "little Dutch boy" or is the hair buzzed up to the middle of the head with the "bowl" starting at about ear-level?

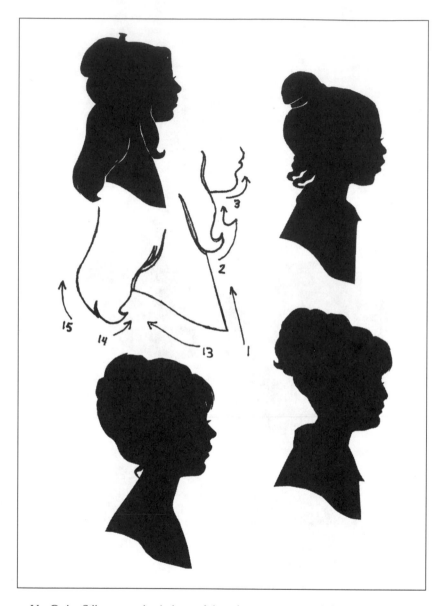

Up-Do's: Silhouettes look beautiful and even more old fashioned when a woman's hair is done up in a bun or some sort of twist. Leave a tendril of hair at the nape of the neck, but otherwise tidy up the bun or up-do for the prettiest effect. A nude neckline is the most classic with the hair done up.

Bobbed hair: Classic bobbed hair-cuts fall somewhere between the upper jaw-line and the bottom of the chin. Reflect the blunt cut and its unique shape by echoing it with a "slice of light." This minimalistic style of embellishment is easily accomplished by simply cutting a hair-thin line out of the black paper where you want that added detail to show. Once the silhouette is pasted down, the white of the background will show through the cutting for a more dramatic and defined effect.

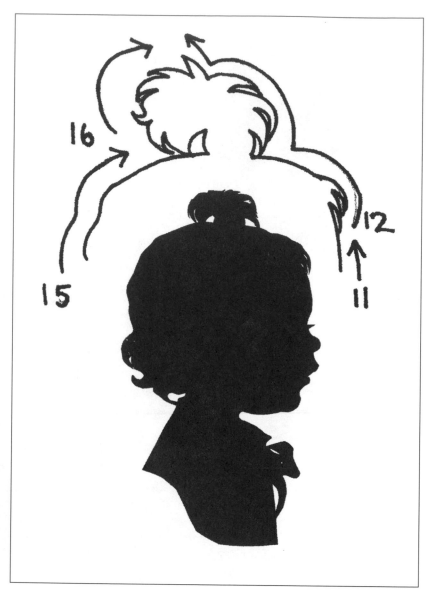

"Fountain" hair: Do the portrait up to the front half sprig of hair. Then proceed as usual to the cameo and work your way up the back of the head. If you measured correctly, everything will meet perfectly at the top of the head as you finish up the sprig.

Braids: Braids translate beautifully into silhouette. Look at the ridges on the braid, paying close attention to the direction of flow and braid length. Is it a thick braid with fat sections or a thin tight braid? Where on the back does it fall?

French Braid: Make the braid as usual, but continue cutting the ridges of the braid all the way up to the top of the head.

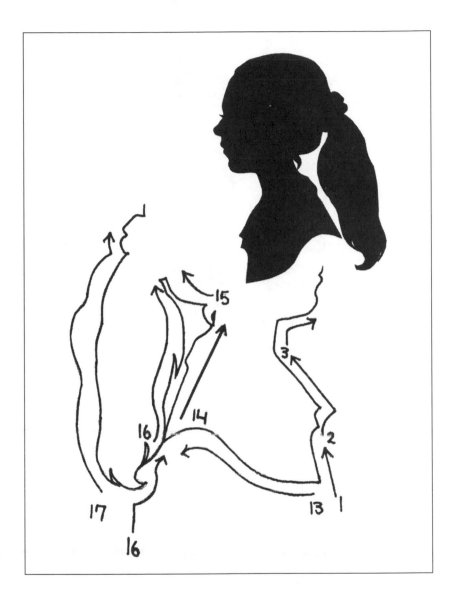

Ponytails: Pay attention to length, flow and thickness of hair, as well as where the pony tail is tied in place on the head. Is it a high ponytail or a low ponytail? Is it straight, wavy or curly? Can you see some space between the ponytail and the head where the ponytail is tied in place? Is half of the hair down with the other half pulled up in a little pony-tail on top of the head?

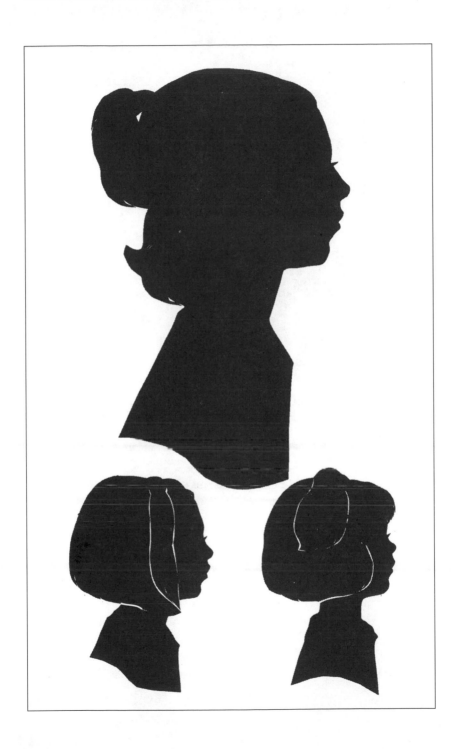

Illustration 1

Illustration 2

Pigtails: Pigtails do not always translate well, as most pigtails fall directly in the middle of the head and cannot "truly" be seen in shadow. If you look strictly at a profile with pigtails, the subject can actually look bald (see illust. 1). You will have to use artistic license and cut into the head to echo the shape of the pigtail. Adding a bow or some form of hair ornamentation is a good idea, and remember to cut a tiny "slice of light" around the pigtail so you can see the hair detail once it is pasted down (see illust. 2). Another alternative is to turn the pigtail into a ponytail instead. Discuss this idea with the subject or the subject's parents if a child is posing.

Bows: Hair ornamentation can reflect whatever the subject is wearing at the time or can be added on by request. Practice these bows and create your own designs. You can get as elaborate as you like and time will allow. Be sure when cutting out your "slice of light" detail that the bow remains attached to some part of the silhouette. You will have a hard time pasting up all those extra little pieces of paper if you cut the bow off entirely.

Be sure
to leave a
connection
piece.

Silhouette by
Irina Zakharova

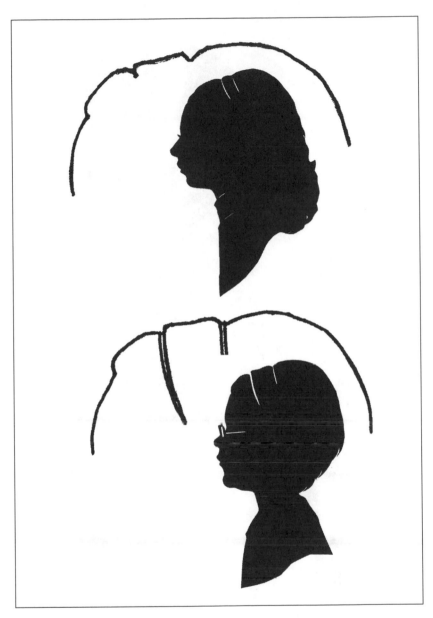

Headbands: Make a ridge at the top of the head indicating the placement and thickness of the headband. Put in detail as the last step by cutting out highlights to show the width of the band.

Hair Clips and Barrettes: Simply reflect the shape of the hair clip or barrette in the silhouette. You may also ask the subject if they would prefer the clip left out, or a bow put in its place instead.

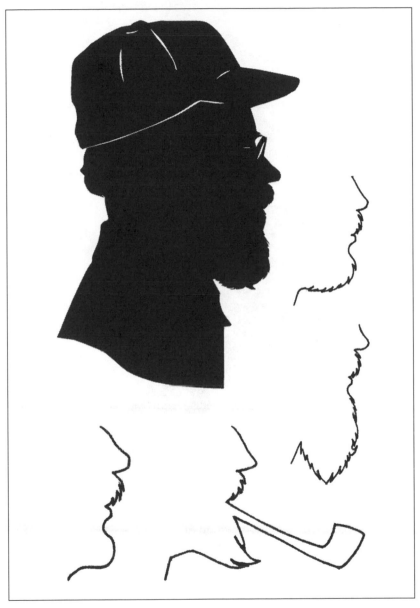

Facial hair: Practice tiny cuts and be sure to follow the shape of the neck and chin carefully when cutting tight beards. The bottom lip usually shows with a beard, but moustaches normally cover the top lip.

Silhouette by
Ed Sanderson

Glasses: These are some extreme close-ups of glasses with the steps to take in numerical order.

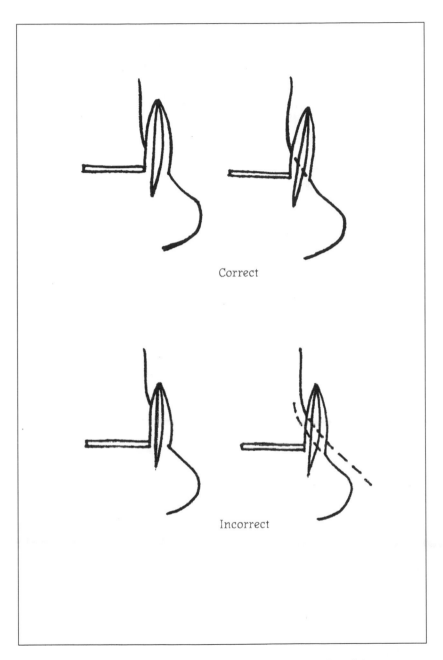

Correct

Incorrect

When making glasses, be sure to follow the line of the bridge of the nose.

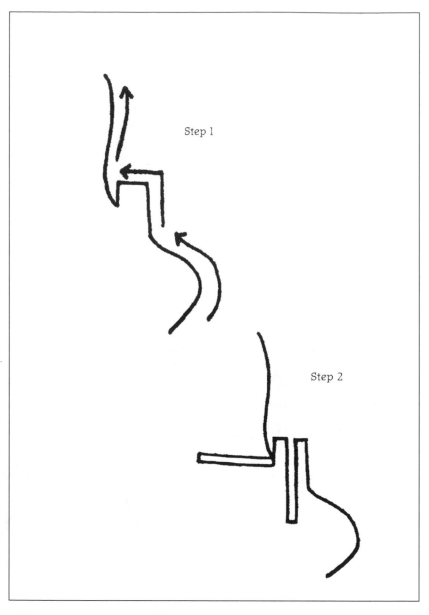

Beginner's glasses with a square lens. Step 1. Cut the nose, the outside shape of the glasses, then up the bridge of the nose to the forehead. Step 2. Cut out a slice notating the lens, then cut a slice denoting the leg of the glasses.

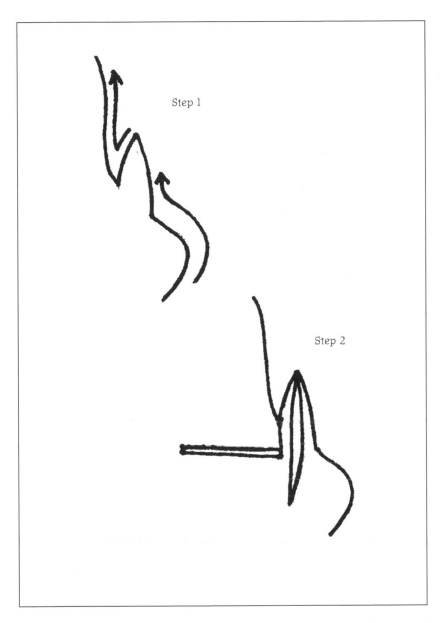

Step 1

Step 2

Beginner's glasses with a curved lens. Step 1. Cut the nose, the outside shape of the glasses, then up the bridge of the nose to the forehead. Step 2. Make a straight cut down, then a curved cut to show a curved lens. Cut the leg of the glasses last.

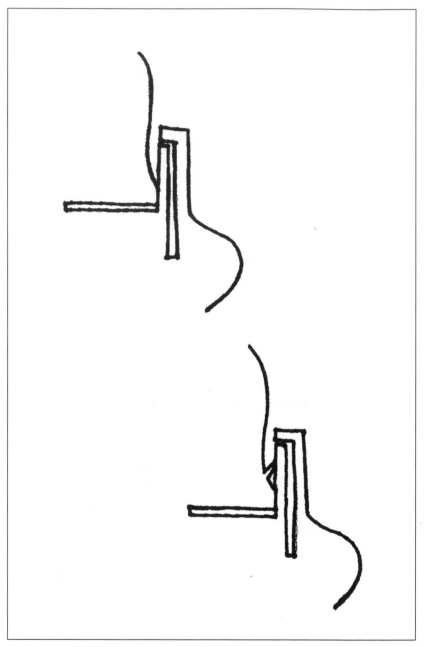

Advanced glasses with a squared lens. Try it with an eyelash!

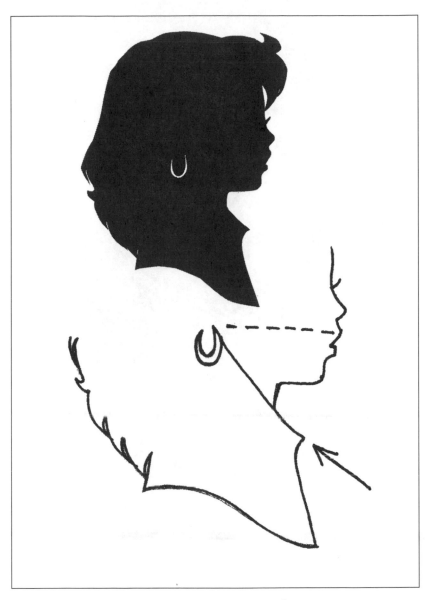

Earrings: Make a cut from the collar to the earlobe (the earlobe lines up across from the top lip), then cut out a "slice of light" in the shape of the earring. Match up the seam when pasting so that a white line doesn't show and give away your little trick.

Hats: For the best results, the subject must be wearing the hat in order for you to see where the hat truly sits on the subject's head. Measure carefully, keeping in mind the parameters of the cranium underneath the hat. Cut the basic outline first, then put in all details as the last step.

The more elaborate the hat or costume, the higher the risk becomes for error. After you cut the basic outline, it is perfectly permissible to lightly sketch in any difficult details that need exact placement on the hat (see page 84). After the details are sketched, simply cut them out without the worry of having to do the portrait over again.

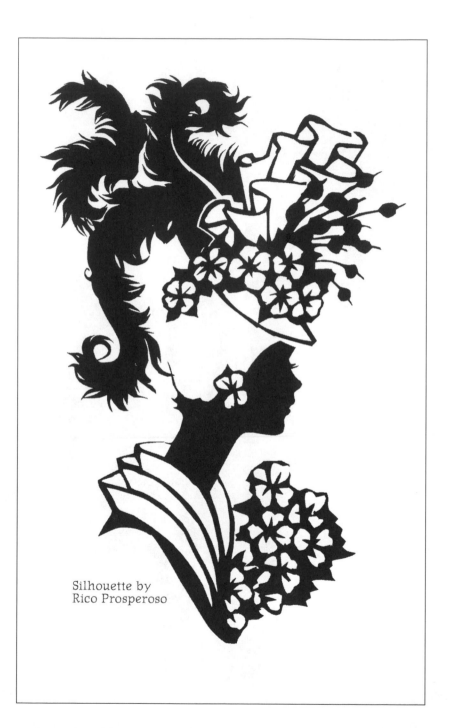

Silhouette by
Rico Prosperoso

Christmas
Card -Cover

Christmas
Card -Inside

Duplication Technique #1. Silhouettes can be photo-copied or scanned and printed out for multiple copies. Silhouettes make beautiful images on homemade holiday cards.

CHAPTER SEVEN
EMBELLISHED SILHOUETTES –
AN ADVANCED TECHNIQUE

Most silhouette artists create their silhouette portraits in a minimalist style with black only, focusing solely on the outline of the subject. This minimalist style of portraiture is faster to cut out, uncluttered and pure. The viewers eyes are left free to focus clearly on the likeness of the subject.

However, another technique used to create silhouette portraits is called the "embellished" style. Embellished silhouettes take added time and engineering to complete and paste down, but this type of silhouette is highly collectable and appreciated for its elegance and added detail. Most people wonder how the artist achieved those tiny cuts inside the silhouette!

When attempting to embellish a silhouette, an artist must strike a delicate balance between graceful and gaudy. An overly-embellished silhouette can be highly distracting as it forces the viewer's eye to jump from place to place all over the portrait. If overdone, a subject can easily become lost in each unnecessary ruffle of the garment and strand of hair. People will surely admire your technique, but will they think it looks like the subject? Will they even notice the subject under all that pomp and circumstance? Don't ever allow embellishment to become a cover-up for a bad likeness of your subject.

Whether you choose to embellish or remain a purist in technique, just remember a simple rule: "less is more." The embellished style looks best on single subject portraits.

Begin by cutting out the silhouette portrait as usual. Next, look at the flow of the hair, as you will want to capture the direction in which it falls or is swept up around the face. Choose your first "entry point" by cutting a seam directly into the silhouette in order to accent a certain area. You may want to follow the natural flow of the hairline down the face and then cut in the fine detail. Cut out slices of light to embellish. Accent the bangs, the collar, a bow, etc. Continue doing this until you are satisfied with the results, without going overboard. Be sure to keep the silhouette connected and in one piece! This will make pasting the portrait down much easier. Unless you look closely, the seams you cut will not show if you paste down the silhouette carefully and burnish delicately.

Step 1: Begin by cutting out the silhouette portrait as usual.

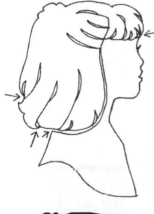

Step 2: Choose "entry points" and cut seams and "slices of light" directly into the silhouette. Be sure to follow the natural flow of the hair.

Step 3: Carefully paste down the finished product.

Step 1

Step 2

Step 3

Step 1

Step 2

Step 3

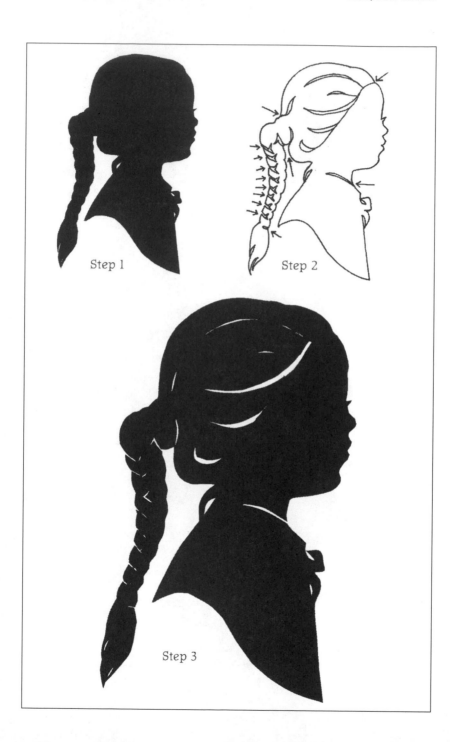

Step 1

Step 2

Step 3

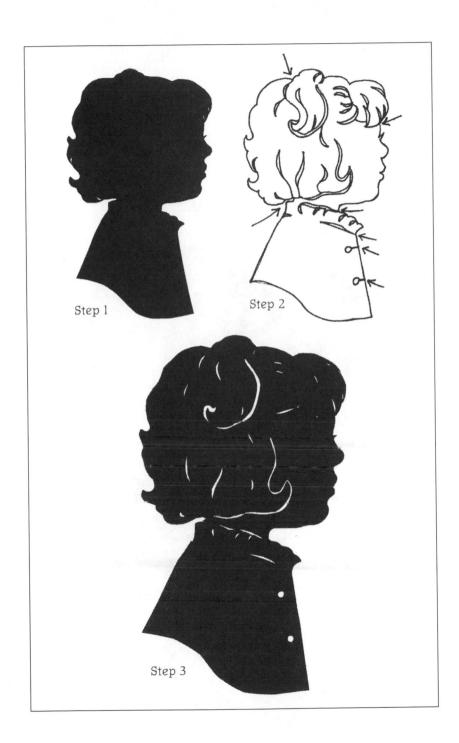

Step 1

Step 2

Step 3

CHAPTER EIGHT
MULTIPLE SUBJECT SILHOUETTES

Master single subjects before moving on to doubles, triples, quadruples, and quintuples. The cutting technique for multiples is the same, but can be perturbing if you do not have the basics down. For example, when making a quadruple (four people in one), if you mess up the fourth person, you must start all over again! But remember, practice makes perfect. With patience and perserverance, you will be less likely to make mistakes.

Silhouette by
Alexandria Skordas

Silhouette by
Vincent Totera

Silhouette by
Vincent Totera

COMPOSITION

Composition is the most important aspect of a multiple subject silhouette. When arranging a group portrait, have all members present. Look at age, height, hair lengths and the gender of all subjects. Each of these factors plays a role in a pleasing composition, and it is up to you to balance them.

1. Age: You can get creative with this part of the composition because it's not as important. For example, you can make the group go from youngest to oldest or vice versa.

2. Height: When making a double, put the tallest subject in the right-most position (illust. 1) unless when showing an attractive hairdo on a female (illust. 2). Show as much of each subject as possible.

3. Hair length: Be careful to compensate for long hair and do not chop off all of the cameo if someone has long hair in the back position (illust. 3).

4. Gender: Gender overrules height and age, and will be the final criterion for the order in which your subjects will appear. If there is a female in the group, always- always- have her sit last for the multiple to showcase her hair (illust. 4). If there are two or more females in a group, be sure to make all of the subjects look feminine by showcasing their hair in some manner (illust. 5). If there are two females, put the taller of the females first to show as much of each person as possible (illust. 6). For long hair, put some hair over the shoulder to show the length and style (illust. 7). For short hair, go back into the picture and echo the hair style by making a cut reflecting the shape of the hair (illust. 8).

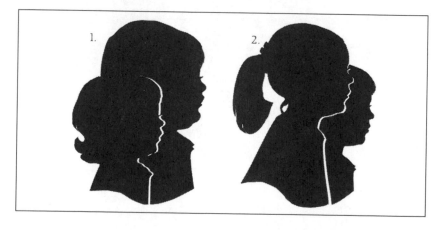

HOW TO CUT MULTIPLES

The following is a step by step example of how to cut a "double" silhouette of a man and woman.

First decide on a good composition (in this case, the man sits first and the woman sits second to show all of her hair). After deciding on the composition, have the first subject sit down. Follow steps 1-12, cutting the portrait up to just past the bangs or to the crown of the head (illust. 9). The first subject is finished, now it is the second subject's turn. The second subject sits, and you cut out their portrait in its entirety right next to the first profile on the same silhouette sheet (illust. 10-12). When the second subject is done, cut the remaining part of the first subject's head to fit against the second subject's head like a puzzle piece (illust. 13).

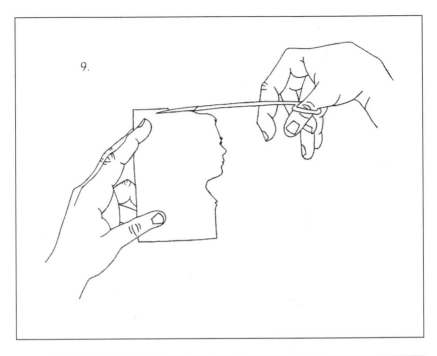

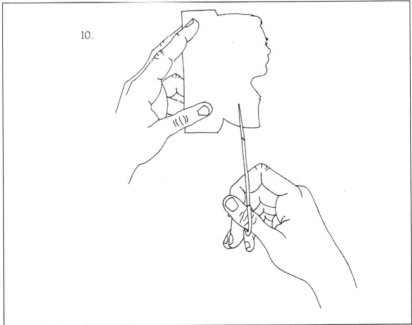

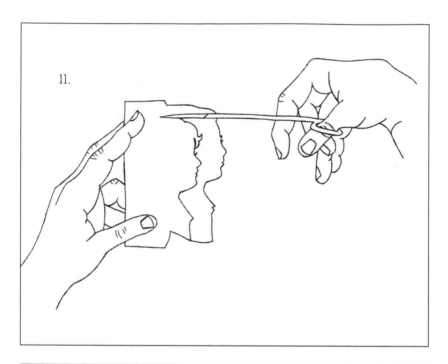

11.

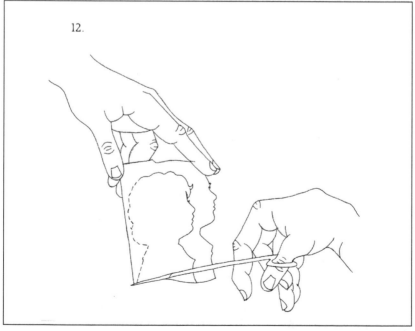

12.

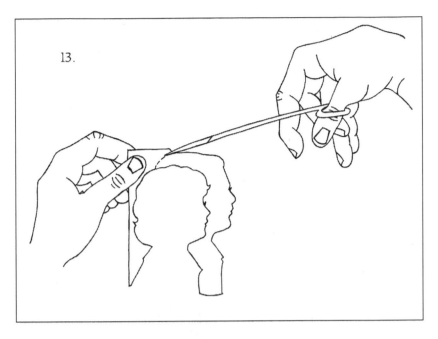

13.

Follow the same principle for triples, quadruples and quintuples.

Remember, if a mistake is made on any member of the group, you must start all over again.

Be sure to keep adequate distance between subjects on the paper. If you cut the subjects too closely together, the risk of cutting a feature directly into a finished subject is higher, thus ruining the entire portrait. You will have to begin again if this mistake is made.

CHAPTER NINE
PASTE-UP AND BURNISHING

Mix a teaspoon of powdered wallpaper paste with some water in the cup until it gets to a medium consistency. Spread a thin coat of paste over a sheet of the white four-ply paper and take the silhouette in your dominant hand. Use your non-dominant hand to steady the paper.

Hold the silhouette 1/2 to 3/4 inch above the pasted paper, and eyeball it in place before setting it on the paper itself. If the silhouette is centered properly, it will fit perfectly in the frame without any of the image getting cut off or being too far over in any one direction.

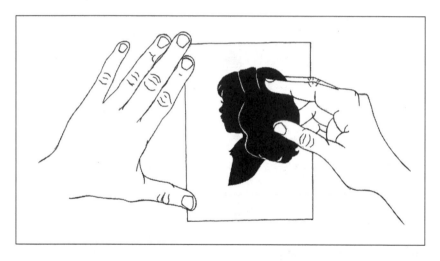

Wallpaper paste is somewhat forgiving. Therefore, if the silhouette is centered wrong on the paper, usually it can be moved with ease before it dries. Try to catch paste-up mistakes as early as possible so they can be remedied quickly without tearing the silhouette. Peel the silhouette off carefully and try centering it again. Paste up one picture at a time for best results.

Spots and Fingerprints. If there are spots or finger-prints on the silhouette after burnishing, put a light coating of wallpaper paste directly on the entire portrait, and burnish again until all the glue is picked up.

This silhouette is perfectly centered.

Do not paste too high or too low.

Do not paste too far to the left or right.

Paste the figure straight, not slanted backwards or forward.

This silhouette
has been pasted
correctly: note the
even space between
both figures.

This silhouette
has been pasted
incorrectly: note
the uneven
space between
both figures.

PASTE-UP FOR MULTIPLES

Practice centering first (place the silhouettes on a sheet of unpasted paper to see where they look best). Place the figure with the whole head first, then fit the other figure(s) around it. Glue the pieces apart by a few millimeters to make white space between the figures, keeping the line as even as possible.

BURNISHING

After centering the silhouette on the pasted 5"x7" mat board, you should smooth it out immediately for best results. This step is called "burnishing." Take a 5"x7" piece of plain newsprint and place it over the pasted silhouette. Take your burnishing tool and softly rub up and down, pressing the silhouette flat while picking up excess glue. (NOTE: See the next page for instructions on how to make this simple tool.)

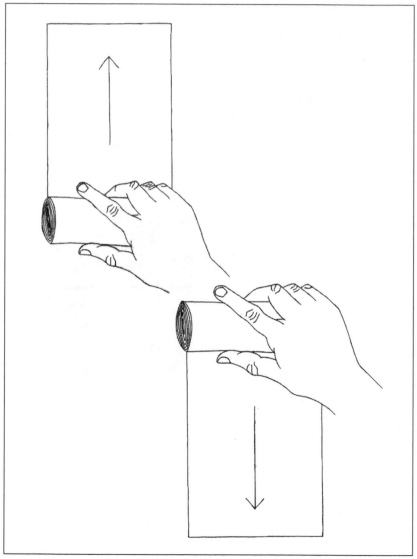

Quickly peel away the newsprint, and the silhouette will be mounted flat. If there are any bubbles or wrinkles, carefully peel back the wrinkled portion of the silhouette, spreading a little glue on the paper and burnishing again. Wipe away any excess glue with newsprint. By this time, the silhouettes are dry and ready to be personalized and framed immediately.

NOTE: How to make the Burnishing Tool

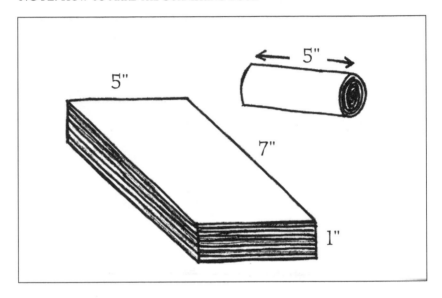

Take a 1" thick stack of plain newsprint (cut 5"x7") and roll it into a tight cylinder. Tape it together with clear or masking tape. Voila! You have a burnishing tool!

Duplication Technique #2. Make a "rubbing" of the silhouette. This technique is for people needing a few duplicates right away. It is also a great save for a ripped silhouette. There is no need to have the person sit again for the portrait. Take a piece of silhouette paper (white side up) and place it over a finished and mounted silhouette (right profile for right handed artists). Next, take a sharpened pencil and turn it on its side. Softly rub the lead over the paper, and the image beneath will appear like magic. Cut out the image.

CHAPTER TEN
PERSONALIZATION

This step is optional. Some artists simply choose to leave the silhouette blank, while others like to sign their work. Some prefer to personalize it with the subject's name and the year. Come up with your own hand-lettering style, or look in calligraphy books and typestyle books for ideas.

Here are some example lettering styles to practice.

Aa Bb Cc Dd Ee
Ff Gg Hh Ii Jj
Kk Ll Mm Nn
Oo Pp Qq Rr Ss
Tt Uu Vv Ww Xx
Yy Zz 1 2 3 4 5 6
7 8 9 0 . , / &

Aa Bb Cc Dd

Ee Ff Gg Hh

Ii Jj Kk Ll

Mm Nn Oo Pp

Qq Rr Ss Tt

Uu Vv Ww Xx Yy

Zz 1 2 3 4 5 6 7 8

9 0 . , / &

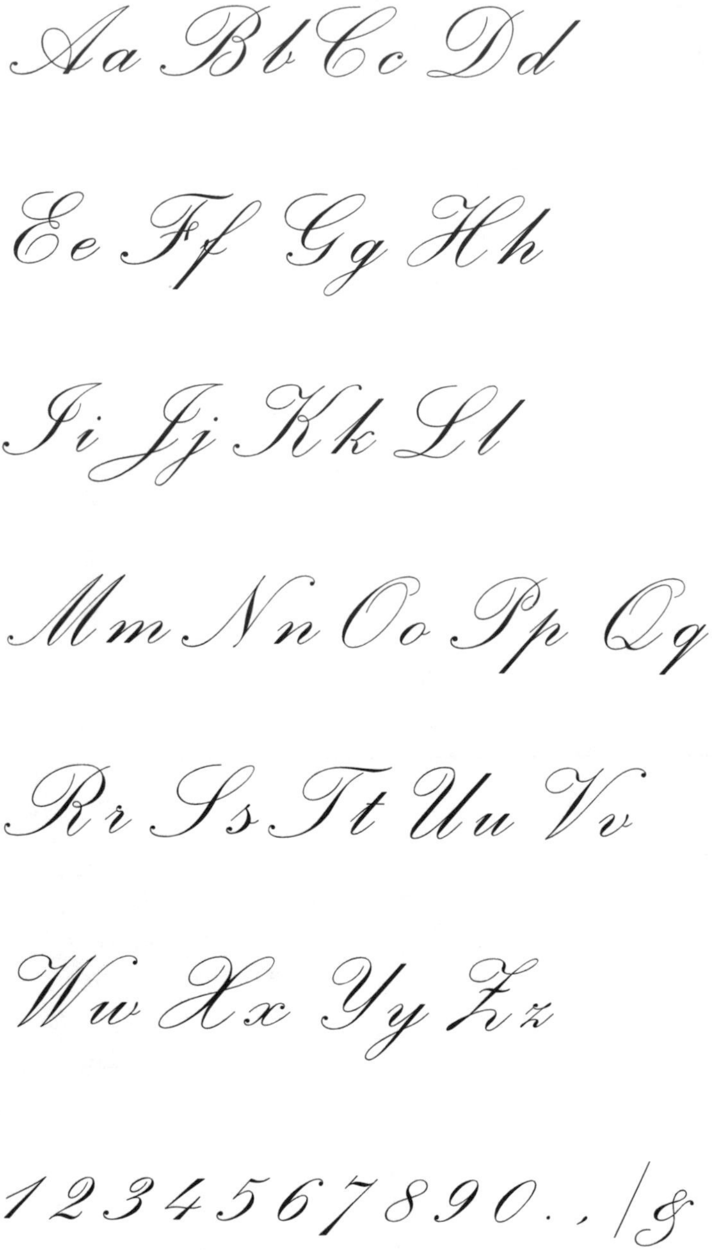

Aa Bb Cc Dd

Ee Ff Gg Hh

Ii Jj Kk Ll

Mm Nn Oo Pp Qq

Rr Ss Tt Uu Vv

Ww Xx Yy Zz

1 2 3 4 5 6 7 8 9 0 . , / &

Aa Bb Cc Dd

Ee Ff Gg Hh

Ii Jj Kk Ll

Mm Nn Oo Pp

Qq Rr Ss Tt Uu

Vv Ww Xx Yy Zz

1234567890 .,/&

$\mathcal{A}$ a $\mathcal{B}$ b $\mathcal{C}$ c $\mathcal{D}$ d

$\mathcal{E}$ e $\mathcal{F}$ f $\mathcal{G}$ g $\mathcal{H}$ h

$\mathcal{I}$ i $\mathcal{J}$ j $\mathcal{K}$ k $\mathcal{L}$ l

$\mathcal{M}$ m $\mathcal{N}$ n $\mathcal{O}$ o $\mathcal{P}$ p

$\mathcal{Q}$ q $\mathcal{R}$ r $\mathcal{S}$ s $\mathcal{T}$ t

$\mathcal{U}$ u $\mathcal{V}$ v $\mathcal{W}$ w $\mathcal{X}$ x

$\mathcal{Y}$ y $\mathcal{Z}$ z   1 2 3 4 5

6 7 8 9 0 . , / &

A a B b C c D d

E e F f G g H h

I i J j K k L l

M m N n O o P p

Q q R r S s T t

U u V v W w X x

Y y Z z 1 2 3 4 5

6 7 8 9 0 . , / &

Below are examples of where to write on singles, doubles, triples, and quadruples. For a simple, uncluttered look, the more people in the group, the less you should write.

Name
Year

Name & Name
Year

Family Name
Year

Here are some ideas of what to write on silhouettes:

First names and the year

Last name and the year

Our Honeymoon (include the wedding month, day, and year)

Our Anniversary (include anniversary month, day and year)

The _____ Family

Sisters

Brothers

The _____ Kids

The _____ Children

The Three Generations (for a Grandmother, Mother, and Daughter)

Location and the year

CHAPTER ELEVEN
FRAMING

After centering and pasting the silhouette, it should fit into any standard 5"x7" frame without any of the image being cut off. Square-shaped or oval-shaped frames work well or the silhouette can be matted and put into a larger frame. When framing a silhouette in an oval-shaped frame, carefully take out the oval-cut glass and place it over the silhouette. Then, centering the silhouette under the glass, lightly trace the outline of the glass onto the paper. Trim around the trace mark and frame the picture. Most frames have enough space in back to store the extra copies for safe keeping.

8x10 mat with a 5x7 opening.

CHAPTER TWELVE
THE BUSINESS OF SILHOUETTES

For the professional, silhouette portraiture can be a very lucrative endeavor. A finished silhouette portrait takes only minutes as compared to the thirty minutes or longer that it takes to complete the average pastel or watercolor portrait. This can translate to a higher volume of customers and increased sales. But, it's important to keep your prices reasonable. Remember, silhouettes are still referred to as the "poor man's portrait."

At first, you may even want to volunteer doing silhouettes for free at local charity events or parties in order to gain the experience of working with the mass public. This experience will increase your confidence, speed and accuracy. I guarantee you, no one will be upset with their silhouette if they don't have to pay for it.

The average silhouette can range from $5.00 up to $20.00 per subject. The price you charge depends largely upon the mastery of your art. *Only a master silhouette artist with a decade or more of experience would likely be able to demand the higher end of this price range.* It's best to start out with low prices. Then, you can gradually increase your prices after you have established yourself and become known for your work.

There are, however, other ways to increase your sales. Framing is an option that most people will want. You can also offer free multiple copies or offer the duplicates at a small discount. People will want to buy the extras so they can give them out as gifts. And, multiple copies mean additional frame sales. An added advantage to making multiple copies is that it's easier to cut two or three layers of paper because the scissors are less likely to slip and rip the silhouette paper as you are cutting.

As you continue to master your skills, it's important to ensure that each portrait you do is of the highest quality possible. Take your time at first and be willing to re-do the portrait until you achieve the results you are going for. Eventually, you will maximize the number of customers you can do in a day, as well as the amount of daily sales you bring in!

MARKETING TIPS

1. Get listed with local talent agencies. They will hire you out for private parties and conventions. Set an hourly rate as your fee, and your agent will tag on their commission accordingly. Keep records of your mileage, food and any other expenses to take off on your taxes. Expect to be paid 30-90 days later for the work, and keep the pay stubs to claim as income on your annual tax return.

2. Get a listing in the yellow pages under "Artists," or "Party Planning" or both. People will call you directly to book you for parties and special events.

3. Go to local preschools and day-care centers. As a gratuity for the school having you there, always give back at least 10% of your total to the school. Create a professional looking flyer to send home with each student. The flyer should include a sample of your work, the price for a sitting, the day you will be at the school, how many copies of the artwork are given, etc.

4. Advertise your services in bridal boutiques and tuxedo shops as an elegant addition to any wedding reception.

5. Do craft shows and festivals. You will need a car large enough to haul all of your supplies, displays, chairs and a tent! A comprehensive listing of upcoming festivals is published monthly by Sunshine Artist Magazine (2600 Temple Dr., Winter Park FL 32789. (800)597-2573).

6. Find a department store in a mall to sponsor you and do a two-day event there by appointment only. Advertise your appearance in the paper.

7. Create a web site offering your services.

More Ideas. For further information on silhouettes, check out your local library or bookstore carrying publications by Dover. Dover publishes copyright free clip art books with scherenschnitte and classic silhouette designs.

CHAPTER THIRTEEN
WORKING WITH CHILDREN

Have a sign that says "We Do Wiggly Kids." This way parents will know that you can do their child's portrait, regardless of age and attention span. When you talk to the parents, stress how quickly the portrait can be completed and always keep a sturdy children's book nearby at all silhouette events you do. A children's book is an invaluable tool, and a "secret weapon" that has a settling effect on a child. Purchase a book with all cardboard pages — lots of pictures — and not too many words. Have the parent show the book at the child's eye level so you can get a good look at the neck and chin area. Make sure the child sits up straight instead of leaning back on the parent.

Children will probably be the highest percentage of your silhouette subjects, therefore, you must be able to work well with them and understand that they usually will not sit perfectly still for you. For starters, they may not want to, or may be scared to. After all, you are a stranger with a big pair of scissors.

You must be sensitive to children while you are working. You will quickly learn how to "read" them, including their moods and temperaments. It is important to make the child feel at ease with you and make them understand that this is something fun and quick.

Take the stress off the child. Smile warmly and show them the children's book. Tell the child to sit with a parent and look at the book for a while. The idea is to divert the child's attention while you cut. Usually by this time the child won't even know you are cutting a portrait.

For the "Looky Lou" child who looks all around or wants to look at you while you are cutting out their silhouette, simply bring the child's attention back to the book by pointing to the interesting pictures. Also, get the parents involved in the process. Have the child sit on the lap of one of the parents while the other holds the book and turns the pages. Tell the parents, "Show them the book, tap on the book, snap your fingers, jingle your keys. Do whatever it takes to have them look straight ahead at the book."

Make sure the child is not eating, drinking, or sucking on a pacifier while making their portrait. These motions will distort the anatomy from the neck all the way up to the nose. Children also do not need to have their hair brushed perfectly, or have their "Sunday best" clothing on in order for you to create an attractive portrait.

Sometimes a parent will ask if you can do the silhouette while the child is asleep in the stroller. The answer is "yes." Simply have the parent carefully prop the child up in the stroller so you can see the child's right profile and begin cutting. In this case, remember to have the head propped so that the neck and chin area aren't distorted. If the child is awake in the stroller, have the parents put the child on their lap. This will help save your back.

Sometimes you will hear a parent say, "Sit still while the lady cuts your face." AAgh! Can you imagine what the poor child must think: "The lady's going to hurt me — she's going to cut my face!" This calls for immediate action on your part. Step in quickly, distracting the child with your book. Make an added effort to hide the scissors until the child feels comfortable. Once you have the child settled with the book, pick up the silhouette paper in your non-dominant hand. Slowly, unobtrusively, pick up the scissors while hiding them behind the paper. Then, engage the child to once again look at the book and begin cutting the silhouette.

When the portrait is completed, always verbally praise the child for doing a good job sitting, or reward the child with a sticker for a job well done.

CHAPTER FOURTEEN
PET PORTRAITS

You can make silhouette portraits of animals from photographs or live sittings. Follow the same basic steps that you would for human subjects, remembering to add bits of fluff and whiskers. Collars with tags, collars with bells, studded collars, bandannas and bows can be added to the portraits to create detail and personality. Use your imagination!

His Imperial
Majesty
Ginsu

Boo-Boo
Kitty

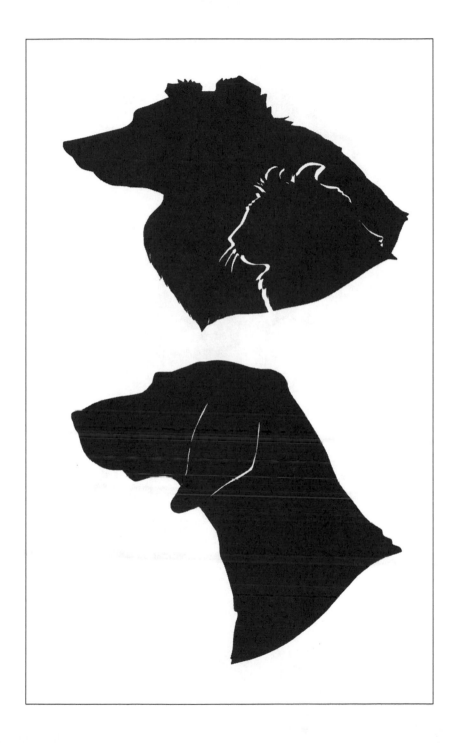

CHAPTER FIFTEEN
TEMPLATES

You may photocopy these silhouettes and practice cutting them out following the steps laid out in Chapter 5. You will find this exercise helpful in furthering your skills with the scissors.

Please be aware that the templates shown in this chapter are for *practice purposes only*, and are not meant for display, publication or resale. Any other use of these templates is strictly prohibited.

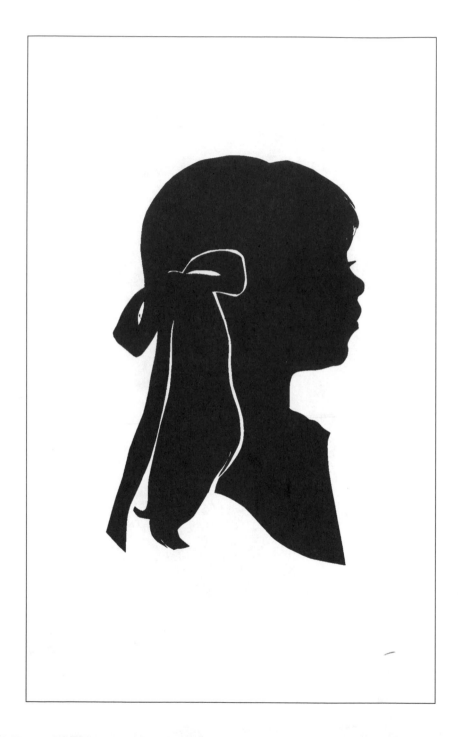

SUPPLIES

- **Scherenschnitte Scissors**
  1 inch blade with 3 1/2 inch shank. Made in Pakistan. Beginner scissors at a beginners price. A decent pair of scissors to see if you're "cut out" for the job!

- **Professional Silhouette Scissors**
  1 inch blade with 5 inch shank. Stainless steel scissors made in Germany. Professional scissors that really get into those nooks and crannies. Excellent control and will last for years before needing to be sharpened. These are the recommended scissors to buy if you want to be a serious silhouette portrait artist.

- **Silhouette Paper**
  Pack of 500 sheets cut to 5x8 inches.

- **White 4-Ply Paper**
  Pack of 500 sheets cut to 5x7 inches.

- **Frames**
  Traditional 5in x 7in black oval frames. These ready-to-hang frames come complete with glass and a cardboard backing.

For a FREE BROCHURE with the latest prices, please write to;
PaperPortraits.com
c/o Kathryn Flocken
P.O. Box 547812
Orlando FL 32854-7812

You may also email me at **kathyart@earthlink.net**, *or visit my web site at* **www.paperportraits.com** *for the most up-to-date prices, specials, new and different artwork, and links to other paper cutters and cool artistic folks to get inspired by!*

INDEX

ABOUT THE AUTHOR

Kathryn Flocken is a professional artist with hands-on experience in a variety of mediums, with emphasis in producing artwork "live and on-stage," including silhouette portraits and paintings. Kathryn has been cutting silhouettes in the Central Florida area since 1989, and has worked throughout all of the WALT DISNEY WORLD Resort theme parks. Along with a Bachelor of Arts in both Communications and Psychology, Kathryn is a self-taught painter and illustrator. Kathryn is presently cutting silhouettes at the Downtown Disney Marketplace, and is one of the featured artists at Orlando's Cafe Tu Tu Tango. Kathryn resides in Orlando with her husband, Berto, and two stepsons.

Ms. Flocken is available for lectures, seminars, training sessions, party bookings and special events. She can be contacted by email at kathyart@earthlink.net or at her Web page www.paperportraits.com

BOOK ORDERS

To order additional copies of this book, please contact me:

BY MAIL: Kathryn K. Flocken
P.O. Box 547812
Orlando FL 32854-7812

BY E-MAIL: kathyart@earthlink.net

ON THE WORLD WIDE WEB: paperportraits.com